Page 7

Pages 10-11

Page 11

Page 12

Page 16

Page 18-19

Page 19

Page 26

Page 28

Page 29

Use these stickers wherever you want!
Can you remember where they are in the book?

Use these stickers wherever you want!
Can you remember where they are in the book?

Use these stickers wherever you want!
Can you remember where they are in the book?

This book belongs to:

- -

- -

I am ☐ years old.

First published by Parragon in 2011

Parragon
Queen Street House
4 Queen Street
Bath BA1 1HE, UK

ISBN 978-1-4454-4066-8

Printed in China

Written by
Sue McMillan
Illustrated by
Sue King

Sophia

Moving Day

PaRragon

Bath • New York • Singapore • Hong Kong • Cologne • Delhi
Melbourne • Amsterdam • Johannesburg • Auckland • Shenzhen

How to use this book

 Read the story, all about Sophia and her first time moving house.

 Look at each picture in the story closely. You may be asked to find or count things in a scene and place a sticker on the page.

 Try each activity as you go along, or read the story first, then go back and do the activities. The answers are at the bottom of each activity page.

 Some pictures will need stickers to finish the scenes or activities. Any left-over stickers can be used to decorate the book or your things.

It's moving day! Sophia feels excited about her new house, but a little sad, too.

FOR SALE

Kitchen

Can you find these things in the picture?

FOR SALE

Kitchen

6

She will miss her old house and her best friend, Michael. He lives next door.

Can you find the teddy in the window?

Place the sticker of Sophia here.

Michael comes to help Sophia finish her packing. "I'll miss you!" he says.

He gives her a card and a gift. "Open it when you get to your new house!"

Colour in Sophia's toys to match the ones in the picture.

Soon it is time to go. "Say goodbye to Michael," says Mum. "I don't want to go," Sophia says. "I'll have no one to play with."

Find 2 stickers to finish the picture.

Can you find these things in the picture?

"You'll make new friends," says Mum.
"And Michael can come and stay."

Place the sticker of Sophia here.

Sophia and her family follow the removal van.
They stop at a restaurant for lunch.

Find 3 stickers to finish the picture.

Which two pieces finish the picture?

 a
 b
 c
 d

After a long drive, they reach the new house. Can you spot five differences in the bottom picture?

Answer

14

Sophia and her brother, Ryan,
race off to explore the house.

"Let's choose our rooms!"
shouts Ryan.

When Sophia and Ryan come back downstairs, the removal men are bringing in the furniture.

Find the sticker of Sophia to finish the picture.

Mum is busy unpacking boxes.
"Time for a break," says Dad.

Help Mum to unpack. Draw lines to join these things with the cupboards where they belong.

Answer

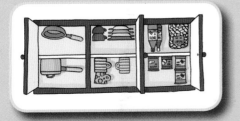

Sophia opens Michael's present. It's a photo.
"I miss Michael," says Sophia.

Find 3 stickers to finish the picture.

Can you find these things in the picture?

Dad sees how sad she is. "Come on,
let's go to the park for a while," he says.

Place the
sticker of
the photo
here.

Help Sophia and her dad find their way to the park.

Answer

It's very quiet at the park. There's just Sophia and another little girl. Dad is talking to her mum.

Can you find 3 butterflies?

Draw yourself sliding down the slide.
Then finish colouring the picture.

The little girl asks Sophia if she wants to play. "My name is Ava," she says.

Find the doll that matches Sophia's doll exactly.

a

b

c

d

e

f

Answer: Doll 'f' matches.

25

When Sophia gets home, she tells her mum about Ava. "I hope I see her again," she says.

Draw lines to join the pairs of shoes that go together. Which shoe doesn't have a pair?

Answer

The next day, Ava comes over with her mum and her baby brother. They have brought an apple pie to welcome Sophia's family.

How many crayons can you count?

Can you find these things in the picture?

Sophia and Ava play while the mums chat.
"I'm drawing a picture of you and me," says Ava.
"And I'm going to draw you!" says Sophia.

Find 2 stickers to finish the picture.

Place the sticker of Ava's picture here.

At bedtime, Sophia's mum sticks Ava's picture on the bedroom wall.

"I'm not sad about moving house any more," says Sophia happily, "because now I have two best friends!"

Point to the thing that's different in each row.

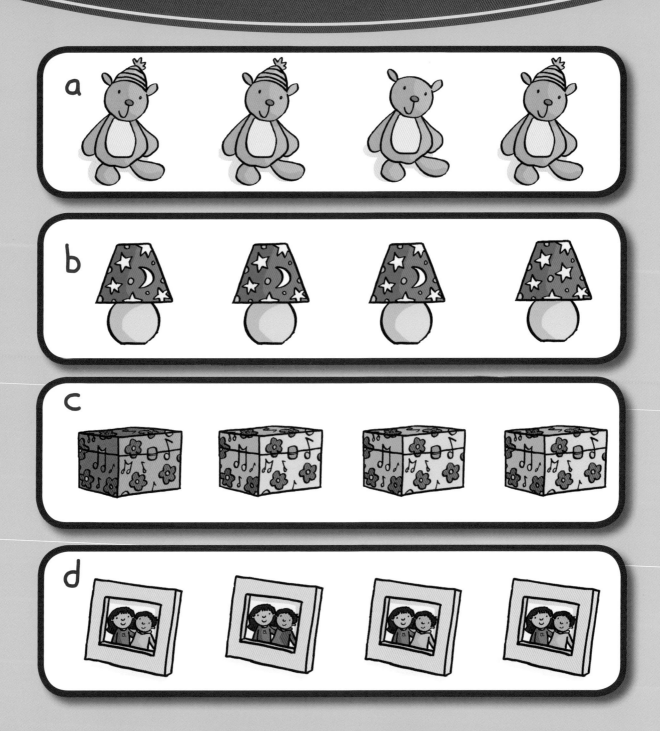

Answers

 d   c   b   a

31

This is to certify that

- - - - - - - - - - - - - - - - - - - -

has been a big help moving
into their new house.

Use your
stickers to
decorate your
certificate.